In the Beginning

The Story of Genesis and Earth Activities for Children

by
Michael J. Caduto

Illustrated by
Adelaide Murphy Tyrol

Peace,

Michael J. Caduto

Paulist Press
New York/Mahwah, N.J.

To God—
With whom all things are possible
through faith, hope, and love

Unless otherwise noted, the scripture quotations herein are from the New Revised Standard Version Bible with Apocrypha, copyright © 1989 by the Division of Christian Education of the National Council of Churches of Christ in the U.S.A. Used by permission.

Jacket design by Sharyn Banks
Text design by Lynn Else

Jacket and interior art copyright © 2004 by Adelaide Murphy Tyrol
Text copyright © 2004 by Michael J. Caduto

Library of Congress Cataloging-in-Publication Data

Caduto Michael J.
In the beginning : the story of Genesis and earth activities for children / by Michael J. Caduto ; illustrated by Adelaide Murphy Tyrol.
    p. cm.
ISBN 0-8091-6717-4 (alk. paper)
    1. Creation—Juvenile literature. 2. Human ecology—Religious aspects—Christianity—Juvenile literature. 3. Bible stories, English—O.T. Genesis. I. Tyrol, Adelaide Murphy. II. Title.

BV651.C33 2004
222'.1109505—dc22

                                                                    2004005819

Published by Paulist Press
997 Macarthur Boulevard
Mahwah, New Jersey 07430

www.paulistpress.com

Printed and bound in Mexico

Contents

Acknowledgments

I would like to thank the staff of Paulist Press for sharing a faith in the importance of this book and for helping to bring it to life: Paul McMahon, Managing Editor, Susan Heyboer O'Keefe, Children's Books Editor, and Lynn Else, Layout & Design Department Manager, for lending a keen eye to fine detail and design. Adelaide Murphy Tyrol's beautiful and evocative illustrations help these stories to sing and come to life. William A. Fletcher refined my handwritten arrangement of the song "'Tis a Gift to Be Simple" and produced the sheet music found within.

My gratitude goes out to the following people at schools, camps, and nature centers for helping to field test and evaluate the stories, reflections, and activities: Ralph Lowder, Director, Anna Carter, Outdoor Educator, and Julia Walsh, Assistant Program Director for Outdoor Education, all of Camp Santa Maria Del Monte in Shawnee, Colorado; Hank Lanik, Director and Sara Schreiber, Ministry Staff of The Pines Catholic Camp & Youth Center, Big Sandy, Texas; and Mildred Alice Levesque of the Espirito Santo School in Fall River, Massachusetts.

Dr. Helen Ross Russell, author, environmental biologist, and consultant and Mildred Alice Levesque, elementary educator, both gave generously of their time in reviewing the entire manuscript. My wife, Marie Levesque Caduto, who is an environmental educator and natural resource specialist, commented on several drafts of the manuscript and was always present with a ready eye and a quick mind. Thank you all for helping me to complete this book and fulfill a longstanding commitment I made ten years ago to both God and myself.

Introduction

Nature is a gift from God. The plants and animals, the rocks, water, and sky enable us to survive and enrich our lives with beauty. The spring of Creation never stops flowing. God "gives rain to the earth and sends waters on the fields..." (Job 5:10).

In the Beginning is a seed to plant and let grow in your heart. It takes you on a journey to new meaning in life. This book will help you to explore the Bible and how it can become a guide for living in a close, connected way with all of Creation. Each chapter begins with a Bible story about Creation that I have chosen and retold in an original version. Although these stories have been adapted, they preserve the details and truths that are found in the Bible.

The stories are followed by reflections. In most cases I have focused on revelations about the nature of Creation and the wisdom that can help to guide our relationship to God's Earth. The reflections also help to connect the stories to the activities that follow.

Activities flow from the subjects found in the stories. Every activity includes a set of simple instructions and a list of the needed materials. These simple materials can be found around the home and/or learning center.

In the Beginning can be read and used directly by children in middle-to-upper elementary level (ages 8 to 12) and beyond. Teachers and parents can read the stories to younger children, answer their questions, and adapt the activities to their levels of understanding. This book can be shared across the generations.

I hope that communities of faith will find *In the Beginning* to be a valuable resource for helping children to see how God's word, and the richness of nature, reveal that every part of Creation is sacred. This book is a guide for people of all ages who want to broaden and deepen the roots of their faith in God, in the natural world, and in humankind.

Creation

(Genesis 1 & 2)

Long ago, at the beginning of time, there was no Sun or Moon, no Earth or Sky. Then God began to create the universe. God made Sky and Earth. On Earth there was no light and a fierce wind howled across the dark waters of a raging sea.

"Let there be light," said God, and light began to shine. Waves gleamed in the first bright rays. "This is good. I will call this light day, and the darkness will be night." That evening the light faded from Sky. Earth returned to darkness.

The light shone on the second day like a fire glowing in Sky. "Now there will be a dome to separate the waters on Earth from the waters above," God declared. Above this dome were the waters of Sky that brought rain and snow. Below it lay the restless oceans. "I will call this arch Heaven," said God.

The next morning, when the light again appeared on Earth, God's words rang out, "I will gather the waters together in places. This way there will be dry land for many living things. These gathering places I will call the oceans and seas."

On the fresh, new soil God sowed the seeds of the first plants. "Grow and bear fruit," God told the plants. "Produce seeds of your own kind so that you may continue to grow." Stems and green leaves sprouted across the new land, bearing flowers of every shape and color and scent. From the flowers came the fruit and seeds of each plant. "This is as it should be," said God, as the light faded from this verdant land.

On the fourth day God said, "Now there will be two lights in the dome of Sky: a warm, bright light for the day and a cool, calm light at night. These lights will separate the light from the darkness." That day, Earth was lit by the light of Sun. "These lights will also be signs of the seasons and the years," said God. "They will mark the festivals and celebrations." After Sun had set, Moon shone down from the night Sky. Countless stars twinkled all through the night.

After Moon went down, and the stars faded in the early morning light of a fifth day, God began to fill the air and the great seas with creatures of all kinds. "Stretch your wings and fly,"

God said to the birds. "Fly through the Heavens and soar across the Sky dome. Make your nests upon the land." Then God spoke to the creatures that swarmed the sea, "Dive and swim in the waters that are your new home." God was filled with joy to see every kind of bird fly through Sky and ring the air with song. As Sun was setting, God's heart leaped with the rise of each whale and rejoiced with the great schools of fish and with the sight of all the creatures of the sea. "Blessed you are," God told them all. "Be fruitful and multiply to fill the land and seas."

In early dawn of the sixth day God continued to fulfill the promise of Creation. "Now the animals will spring forth from Earth," said God. "From Earth will come the sheep and cattle, the lions and wild dogs, the snakes, lizards, turtles, and frogs. Insects will feed on the nectar of flowers." When the land, the air, and waters were streaming with life, God was pleased. Earth was alive with the richness of nature and the seas overflowed in their abundance. Flocks of birds filled the air, pods of whales and schools of fish swam the waters, padded feet walked on Earth, while strange creatures burrowed through the living soil.

Now God reached down and took up a bit of Earth. From this dust God created the first man and woman. God breathed into their nostrils and they came to life. "Blessed are you," said God. "See above you the birds in Sky. There before you are the fish in the seas, the whales and porpoises that play in the waters I have created. Surrounding you is a multitude of creatures that slither and gallop across the land. The trees and all of the green plants are my gift of food to the gazelle, to the birds of Heaven, to the humming insects, and all of the wild animals."

"Go forth and multiply on Earth," God said to the first people. "In your abundance, take care of this sacred garden, the wild beasts of the air and sea, and every living creature that moves upon the land. I have created for your food the living plants and their seeds and every tree that bears fruit and seeds." Then Sun set on another day that saw the flowering of Earth.

On the seventh day God rested and said, "Blessed be this day, a day of holiness. This shall be a day to give thanks for the beauty and wonder of Creation."

Reflections

Genesis comes from the Greek and Latin words that mean "birth" and "origin." Wisdom is the first thing that God gives to the universe (Prov 8:22–31). Then, Creation is born from God's goodness (Prov 3:13–20). Earth and Sky, day and night, Sun and Moon—everything God makes has its opposite. When each of the two are put together, they are complete (Sir 42:24–25).

God creates the animals of land and sea and the birds of Sky in all their splendor and tells them to grow and produce more of their kind. Earth becomes a place of beauty, richness, and abundance. In their joy, all of Creation sings praises to God—from the angels and stars, the fire and frost, to the birds and whales (Song of Thr 35–59, from the Apocrypha). The Heavens tell of the beauty of God's Creation. Day speaks to day and night speaks to night. Although their song is silent, it can be heard all around the world (Ps 19:1–6).

People are made from soil—the very dust of Creation. We are given everything we need to survive: "…water and fire and iron and salt and wheat flour and milk and honey, the blood of the grape and oil and clothing" (Sir 39:26). God breathes more than just life into these first human beings. They are given a purpose: to care for all of Creation. God gives people dominion over Creation, a word that, throughout the Bible, is part of the covenant with God that places Creation into our care. It calls upon us to practice wise stewardship, to serve God and nature and to treat them respectfully. God gives people the responsibility to watch over and nurture the world around them.

After the great flood, God makes a promise to Noah and his people: "As long as the earth endures, seedtime and harvest, cold and heat, summer and winter, day and night, shall not cease" (Gen 8:22). We, too, can sing songs and praises to Yahweh. We can sing from the tops of the mountains and from the deepest valleys to give thanks for the wonders of Creation (Isa 42:10–12; Ps 95:1–7).

Activities

Everything we receive is a gift. We can show our gratitude by taking only what we need and not wasting. This is a way to show respect for all of God's Creation. It is good to treat the rest of nature as a living thing, to ask God's permission before taking anything, and to show appreciation by returning gifts of our own to the forest, sea, desert, or wherever we happen to be.

The Gift of a Sacred Place

MATERIALS: Pencils, chalk, charcoal or pastels, pad to write on, cushions or blankets to sit on, small flat stone, smooth piece of wood or bark, music and lyrics for the song "'Tis a Gift to Be Simple."

Travel with your friends, family, or classmates to a beautiful place in nature. Take a walk by the seashore, atop a hill or mountain, deep in a forest, along the edge of a marsh, out in the wide open desert or plains, deep in the rows of a cornfield, in a city park, or even in the quiet corner of an old cemetery. Bring a pencil, a piece of chalk, a bit of charcoal, or some pastels, and a cushion or blanket on which to sit. If you cannot travel to a natural environment nearby, imagine you are in a favorite place of yours, like a field, lake, or the beach.

Once you arrive in your sacred place, look around for a small flat stone or a smooth piece of wood or bark. Find a comfortable spot; sit quietly for a time and think about what attracts you to that special place. Is there an old tree that draws you in close to it? Do you like the sound of waves breaking on the shore or the rush of wind through the branches? Is there a big, open sky stretched out before you, or a beautiful view? Do you see and hear bird songs?

Give thanks for those things that you love about your sacred place. Pick up the writing or drawing materials you brought with you and the smooth rock, bark, or wood that you gathered. Draw a picture or create a poem upon its surface to express your gratitude to God and your sacred place—to say "thank you" in your own original way.

Try your hand at writing haiku. A haiku is a short poem that has three lines and does not rhyme. Starting with the first line, the numbers of syllables per line are five, seven, and five.

Here is an example of a haiku:

windy waving leaf
you flutter like a feather
on the wings of trees

After everyone is finished, gather in a circle with the rest of your group. Read again the story retold here from Genesis about how Earth and all life were created by God. Open the circle for a time so that anyone who wishes can share what he or she has created for giving thanks. And after the sharing, take time for all to give their Creations as a gift to that place. Return the part of nature that you gathered back to the same place where you found it. Lay the bark, wood, or stone against the soil with your writing or artwork facing down. Or, if you are down by the shore, gently toss your stone into the water.

Then, you can all say, "Thank you, God, for the wonder of this place and for all of your many gifts. With these presents we give something back to you!" Finish your visit by singing the song "'Tis a Gift to Be Simple."

'Tis a Gift to be Simple

Composed by the Alfred Ministry
June 28, 1848

Arrangement by Michael J. Caduto

'Tis a gift to be sim - ple, 'tis a gift to be free, 'tis a gift to come down where we ought to be, and when we find our- selves in the place just____ right 'twill be in the val - ley of love and de - light. When true sim - pli - ci - ty is gain'd, to bow and to bend we shan't be a- sham'd. To turn, turn will be our de - light 'til by turn - ing, turn - ing we come round right.

Creating Creation

MATERIALS: Pencils, lined paper, crayons or colored pencils, construction paper, water colors, brushes, containers of water, old newspapers to work on top of, and rags for cleaning up.

Pretend that someone has asked you to create the universe. What would you include? What would you leave out? How would your Earth look different from the one we live on today? Make two lists: (1) a list of what you want in your universe, and (2) a list of what you do not want there.

This may sound simple at first, but you will have to think hard about what role everything plays in your universe. For example, maybe you think earthworms are creepy. Then you have to consider how important they are for helping to create and fertilize the soil that grows our food and the food that feeds the animals. Every time you leave something out, you must first learn what that would cause to happen in your universe.

Once you have completed the lists of things you would include, and of the things you would leave out, draw a picture of your universe.

After you have completed your illustration, sit and study it for a time. Imagine living in that world. Write a story about a day in your universe. Be sure to put into the story all of those things you included in your world.

Noah and the Great Flood

(Genesis 6–9)

Long ago, when life was new, giants called Nephilim lived among the humans. These enormous, powerful beings did many heroic deeds for humankind. Back in those early days people, too, began to multiply and spread throughout Earth. But human beings had evil thoughts, and they lived in ways that displeased God.

"I am sorry that I ever created these wretched people!" God cried out. "My heart aches to see them living such corrupt and violent lives. Noah is the only one among them who has a kind heart. He treats others fairly and his life is just. The rest of humankind I will wipe off the face of Earth!"

God came to Noah and said, "I am going to destroy this violent world and all of the people within it. I will flood all of Creation beneath angry waters, cold and deep. Everything that breathes with the spirit of life will die."

Noah shuddered and asked, "And what of my family?"

"Do not fear," answered God. "With you, I will form a covenant. You and your loved ones will be safe. But there is much work to be done."

"What must I do to save them?" asked Noah.

"Go and build an ark with three decks and a roof. Cut the ribs from the wood of the cypress tree and fashion the hull from mats of reeds. Seal both the inside and outside with pitch to keep out the water. When it is finished, the ark will measure three hundred cubits long, fifty cubits wide, and thirty cubits high. From top to bottom the roof will have a drop of one cubit. Build a large door into the side of the ark."

"What will I use this door for?" Noah asked.

"Before I send the flood waters down upon Earth, your family will enter the ark by these doors: you, Noah, and your wife, then your sons Shem, Ham, and Japheth, and your sons' wives."

"The ark will be far too large for such a family," Noah observed.

"It will be a magnificent ark," God agreed, "an ark to keep your family and all of my wild creatures and plants safe from the raging waters. In seven days the rain will begin to fall, day and night. In these seven days you must build the ark. When it is completed, you and your family must lead two of every kind of wild beast aboard, both a male and female of each animal and bird, every kind of reptile, and every being that I have made. Bring seven pairs of every bird and animal that is clean according to my customs, and one pair of all the others. Load and store enough of every kind of plant and every food that exists: enough for you and the wild creatures to survive for many months."

Noah and his family began to do what God asked. As they cut the reeds, felled the trees, and shaped the boards for the ark, the sound of their axes rang across the land. The people of that region who heard of the ark came to watch and wonder as the gigantic craft took shape. Planks were fashioned and bent around the massive timbers, forming ribs in the belly of a colossal wooden creature made for the sea.

Darker and more ominous grew the skies until the clouds hung as billows of slate. Two by two the animals and birds and all creatures that crawled were led into the ark. Lightning flashed and thunder rocked the heavens, just as God commanded.

The seventh day dawned on Noah and his family leading the multitude up a ramp and into the belly of the ark. Noah's wife sowed the seeds of every kind of plant in the garden that she would tend when the ark was afloat. Here, over the coming months, she would nurture the families with her growing green lives—the plants that would provide food for all living things.

On the seventh day of the second month, in Noah's six hundredth year of life, the sky split open and poured a rain such as no one had ever seen. The springs and rivers, lakes and ponds overflowed and began to fill the oceans. When the ark was fully loaded with the Lord's precious living cargo, God closed the door and sealed it against the flood.

Day after day the rain fell in an endless curtain. The swelling ocean lifted the ark. Rolling and rocking, it was driven by wind and waves. Over and over its great prow rose upon the crest of a giant wave, tipped, and slid down into a valley surrounded by steep slopes of water. In time, even the mountaintops were swallowed up by a vast sea that rose fifteen cubits above the tallest peaks.

Safely inside the ark, Noah and his family grieved for the many lives lost to the rising flood: friends, other members of their families, and countless strangers. Cattle drowned, as did the

reptiles, the insects, and all of the wild animals that remained on land. Birds flew and cried out to the dark, rainy skies, only to tire at last and plunge into the mouths of hungry waves.

Wind rushed over the roof of the mighty ark, washing the decks with spray that smelled of salt. Days and weeks passed until the ark had been afloat for a full cycle of the moon. But still the rains fell. Forty days passed, and the rain continued.

When it had rained for one hundred and fifty days, God remembered Noah and the precious life that was tossing in the ark's hold. A clearing wind began to rise and beams of light shone down from a break in the clouds. Springs stopped feeding the flood and the waters began to ebb. For one hundred and fifty days the oceans receded. Ten months after the storm had begun, mountaintops again began to shimmer in the sunlight.

Noah opened the trap door on top of the ark and let a raven fly out as he said, "Go and find a place where we may come to ground." But the tireless bird remained in flight from that day forth, searching for dry earth.

Seven days later, Noah released a dove to search for land, yet the bird found nothing but restless seas. Weary, it returned to Noah's hand.

Another seven days passed, and Noah again released a dove to search for a place to come ashore. Late that day, as the sun was setting, the dove returned holding a leaf from an olive tree in its beak. Seven days later, Noah set the dove free once more, but she did not return.

"Land!" cried Noah. "The beautiful dove has found a home!"

Everyone rejoiced when they heard the good news. The sounds of singing and dancing echoed in the hold of the ark.

At last, the ark ran aground on the slopes of a mountain in Ararat. On the day when Noah reached the age of six hundred and one, he threw off the hatch of the ark and found that the land was dry.

But Noah and all aboard the ark waited patiently for God's word to come. A month passed, and another twenty-seven days went by before God spoke to them. "It is time to leave the ark, Noah. Go, tell everyone to come out: your wife, your sons, and their wives. Lead the animals out onto the land. Free the birds and beasts so that they may spread across the face of Earth to feed in the wild, to grow and multiply.

Noah and his family did as God said. They led every kind of creature from the ark. Galloping, walking, crawling, and flying came the families of camels, cattle, lions, birds, reptiles, worms, and insects. Elephants bellowed their freedom while birds circled in the sky and sang with joy.

When at last the ark was empty, Noah peered into the vast hold and thought of the long journey they had completed. He walked out onto the deck and felt the warm rays of sunlight that were casting golden hues across a land alive and green with life.

At that moment, Noah's heart was filled with gratitude for the safe passage God had granted him and his intrepid travelers. There, on the slopes of a mountain in Ararat, Noah built an altar and made a sacrifice of birds and animals that had been cleansed and blessed.

When God saw what Noah was doing and smelled the blood of the animals upon the altar, God felt compassion. "Now, it is done," God said. "The curse is forever lifted. No matter how evil the thoughts and deeds of humankind may be, even in the tempest of youth, I will never again kill people, or any life on Earth. The rainbow in the clouds will be a symbol of my covenant with you and your people, with all those children yet to be born, and with every living thing on Earth."

As long as Earth shines,
　　the planting and the harvest will never cease—
　　　　cold of winter and heat of summer,
　　　　dark of night and light of day,
　　　　these Circles all, shall ever turn.

Reflections

Noah has been chosen because his heart is pure and his life has followed the teachings of God. His reward—a thing of honor—is to be put in charge of saving all of life on Earth from a great flood. We can only imagine how such a burden must have felt.

After the storm is over and the flood has passed, God makes a covenant with Noah and all his descendants. God promises never again to cause a flood on Earth, to kill all of the animals, or to harm humankind, even if people give in to the forces of evil. The rainbow becomes a sign of God's covenant with Earth (Gen 9:13–17). Noah has complete faith in God's words and deeds.

Every species of plant and animal has its own specific needs in order to survive: clean air and water, food, shelter, and habitat in which to live. As the guardians of life on Earth today—the Noahs of our time—it is up to us to make sure that humankind and all of Creation are able to survive and coexist. In smaller ways, our own faith in God calls each of us to protect Creation. In time, our lives will be the measure of how well we loved and cared for God's wonders.

Job tells us God is proud of the animals. The amazing diversity of animal life on Earth is a sign of God's greatness: the animals' songs, their different sizes, the many ways they survive in every kind of habitat, from parched deserts to oceans vast and deep.

In God's house, even the sparrow found a home and the swallow a nest for herself and her young at God's altars (Ps 84:3). Animals speak to us through their actions, through their voices and songs, and by how they use symbolic shapes and colors. We only need to train our ears to listen, our eyes to see, and our hearts and minds to understand. If we want to learn about God and the wonders of Creation, we can ask the wild animals to teach us and ask the birds to tell us. The fishes of the sea will show us. Earth itself will declare that God has made all of these things. God holds the souls of every living thing and the breath of every person (Job 12:7–10).

Activities

These activities are based on the wisdom of the ark as a symbol of the stewardship and protection of all life. They are a way to honor all of Creation, especially those plants and animals that are in the greatest need of our support and protection.

Arks of Life Around Us

Go to a park, nature center, preserve, or zoo to see and learn about some of the animals that live in your area.

Start doing things to help the animals around you. Some excellent books to use as guides for helping wildlife include *Gardening for Wildlife: How to Create a Beautiful Backyard Habitat for Birds, Butterflies and Other Wildlife* by Craig Tufts and Peter Loewer (National Wildlife Federation and Rodale Press: Emmaus, Pennsylvania, 1995); *Garden Birds: How to Attract Birds to Your Garden* by Dr. Noble Proctor (Rodale Press, 1998); and *Butterfly Gardens: Luring Nature's Loveliest Pollinators to Your Yard* by Alcinda Lewis (Brooklyn Botanic Garden: New York, 1997).

Here are some projects you can do at home:

- Put up a bird feeder

- Put up some nesting boxes for birds

- Put up a roosting box for bats

- Plant some flowers to feed and attract butterflies and hummingbirds, or plant some berry-bearing bushes for birds

- Get involved in the local chapter of the Audubon Society, or some other conservation group that works to help or protect local animals

Build Your Own Ark of Life

MATERIALS: Large piece of brown packing paper or pieces of construction paper, tape, stapler, crayons, scissors, paste, and photographs or illustrations from books and magazines of the animals you choose. *Alternative activity: add egg cartons, Popsicle® sticks, clay.*

Hang a large piece of brown packing paper on a wall or set up a backdrop on a bulletin board by joining pieces of construction paper. Use crayons or sculpted pieces of construction paper to create a mural—a giant silhouette of an Ark of Life.

Now find or draw pictures of the animals you are helping, or find or take their photographs. Cut out these images and paste them inside the Ark of Life.

Alternative activity: Use egg cartons or other empty containers adorned with Popsicle® sticks as miniature arks and place tiny animals inside that are made from clay or paper cut-outs.

Expand this activity and do something to help save an endangered animal—a species that is so rare it could easily be wiped out completely.

STEWARDSHIP FOR YOUR ARK OF LIFE

- Don't buy food, leather, or other things that come from endangered species.

- Encourage your parents and friends to drink only coffee that comes from shade-grown coffee beans. The forests in these habitats support many different kinds of animals. Coffee that comes from plantations containing nothing but coffee plants takes the place of animals' homes in that area.

- Convince adults to only buy wood and things made from wood that come from forests grown and harvested so as to protect the plants and animals living there. Look for a sticker that says the wood, or things made from wood, such as furniture, were approved by the Forestry Stewardship Council and the SmartWood program of the Rainforest Alliance.

- Join and donate your time to help conservation groups that work to protect animals, such as the World Wildlife Fund, the National Wildlife Federation, the Audubon Society, and the Humane Society.

- When you hear that something is going to be built where a rare species lives, get some people together and try to either stop the development, get the developers to protect that species' habitat, or get local conservation groups interested in protecting that habitat and possibly even buying the land.

- Let other people know when you learn about an animal that needs help: write to the newspaper, call local radio and television stations, and post reports on your own website or that of your school.

- Do everything you can to save water and energy, to use less paper and other resources, and to reduce waste by reusing things and recycling. Every one of these actions puts less demand on the environment, reduces pollution, and helps to preserve habitat for animals.

- Ask your teachers and parents to help you find the names, addresses, and websites of the elected government officials in your city or town, as well as those in the federal government. Write to these officials. Ask them what they are doing to enact and enforce laws to protect wild animals. Ask them how you can help.

- Before acquiring a pet, ask yourself: Am I meant to keep part of God's Creation in captivity? What about the life it would lead in the wild, including the young that it would produce? How would I feel if I were in that animal's place?

- If you still *really* want to get a pet, don't buy or collect an animal or plant unless you have written proof that it was bred and raised in captivity. Most but not all animals that are sold in pet stores come from far away. Many animals and plants have become rare and endangered because too many of them have been taken and sold, often by poachers.

- Pick a particular endangered animal or plant that you care deeply about. Do all that you can to help save that species.

More Activities

Everything comes from God and something of God's creative spirit dwells in all forms of life. We speak to people because they look and sound like us, but why not communicate with the rest of God's Creation? Lions, cats, dogs, birds, horses, pigs, cows, goats, sheep, and other animals speak to us all the time. They use their voices and body language. We respond by saying their names, by using the tone of our voice, and by touching them in certain ways.

First is a puppet play about listening to the animals.

Listen to Lion and Lamb

MATERIALS: Copy of script for the puppet play *Listen to Lion and Lamb*, construction paper, pencil, cardboard, crayons, scissors, glue, tape, pictures of each animal to use as models for the puppets, sticks on which to mount the puppets, table and old blanket or sheet for puppet stage, and props for the stage set (a few forest trees, apple tree and apple, etc.).

Narrator: One day long ago, Lamb fell asleep in the sun. When she awoke after a long sleep, her flock was gone and she was all alone. "Baaah!" cried Lamb as she searched for her flock. "Baaah!" But Lamb became lost and wandered down a dark trail through the forest. Lion was walking up the same trail toward Lamb, but each did not know that the other was there. Suddenly, they came around a bend and almost ran into each other.

Lion: *(Baring his sharp teeth)* Rooarrr!

Lamb: *(Flicking her ears and jumping about on her feet)* Baaah!

Lion: What are you so afraid of?

Lamb: I am not afraid!

Lion: *(Sarcastically)* Yeah, right.

Lamb: Why do you lions always have to pick on someone half your size?

Lion:	I'm a lion and you're a lamb. I'm supposed to eat you.
Lamb:	I never did anything to you!
Lion:	And I'm not really interested in eating you! Things are this way because of those human beings. It's all their fault. It was their idea that we should be enemies. And it all happened because they don't listen and can't understand a word we say.
Lamb:	I know what you mean. Whenever my keeper sees me wagging my short tail, he thinks I'm the most faithful animal around. But, mostly, I'm just trying to tell him I'm hungry, or that I want to play. Why don't they understand us?
Lion:	Well, it all started a long time ago.
Lamb:	What started?
Lion:	Many years ago…
Lamb:	How many years?
Lion:	…back in the beginning of time, everyone lived together peacefully in a beautiful garden called Paradise. People and animals could understand each other just fine.
Lamb:	Then what happened?
Lion:	Someone had to go and eat that nice, juicy apple!
Lamb:	What apple?
Lion:	Don't you know anything?
Lamb:	Not much—I was only born a few weeks ago.
Lion:	Yes, of course. So let me tell you the story. There was an apple tree in the garden. God said that no one should eat the fruit or it would mean the end of Paradise. But those human beings just *had* to take a bite.
Lamb:	Then what happened?
Lion:	One minute we're all getting along fine and can understand each other, the next thing you know, human beings are acting like they've never heard our language before. Then they start chasing us around, hunting us, and cooking us for dinner!
Lamb:	Why didn't someone tell them to stop before they picked the apple?
Lion:	One of the Lions tried to tell them, but they wouldn't listen. One moment everything was fine in the world, then the apple was bitten and it all changed.
Lamb:	Is that when Lambs and Lions became enemies?

Lion: Exactly. But human beings still talk about how, some day, it will be Paradise all over again. You've probably heard them saying, "One day, the lion will lie down with the lamb...blah, blah, blah." They need to learn how to listen to the animals again, to stop eating those forbidden fruit, and to *get real!*

Lamb: I know how the humans must feel, though. *(A bird calls in the distance)* I don't really understand the language of the birds, or the insects, or even the songs the frogs sing.

Lion: Me neither. Ever since that day, animals only seem to understand the other animals that look a lot like them. You know, whether they have the same number of legs or eyes, fur or feathers, a tail—that sort of thing. *(Mouse comes creeping up toward Lion and Lamb)*

Lion: *(Looking at mouse)* What are you so afraid of?

Mouse: *(Shaking)* Y–y–you're the biggest cat I've ever seen!

Lion: Don't worry, you're hardly big enough for a snack.

Mouse: Thanks a lot! I may be small, but there's no need to be insulting.

Lion: Whoa, down Mousey. I'm sorry!

Mouse: Who are you calling *Mousey?* Anyway, I've been hiding under that leaf over there for quite a while, listening to both of you.

Lion: And?

Mouse: I wish we could go back to the days when nobody hunted at all. Hardly anyone knows my language because I only get to talk to other mice. I have to run away and hide every time I see someone coming.

Lion: You mean, like me?

Mouse: Did you need to ask?

Lamb: And me? Do you run away when you see me coming?

Mouse: Well, no. Maybe if I were a blade of grass I would run away from you. I don't think *anybody's* afraid of *you,* Lamb. *(In the distance, another animal slithers toward the three of them)*

Lion: Who's that over there?

Mouse: Well, it has a long body and a forked tongue and is covered with scales. I think it's a–a–A SNAKE! *(Mouse disappears into the leaves while Lion and Lamb stand there and watch as Snake gets closer)*

Lion: I think Mouse is right. In fact, judging by its markings I would say that Snake is a deadly poisonous viper.

Lamb: And what do you think we should do?

Lion and Lamb: *(Lion and Lamb slowly look at each other, then look back at the viper, and both scream)* RUN AWAY!!! *(Both exit)*

Speak to the Animals

MATERIALS: Lined paper, construction paper, pencils, or crayons.

Pick a common wild animal around your house, such as a robin, a squirrel, or a deer. Watch that animal's actions, listen to the sounds it makes, and try to interpret its language. What is it showing and saying to others of its kind? What kinds of messages is it giving to other animals, or to people when they come too close? Why does a squirrel make a loud sound and flick its tail when you come near? Why do deer, buffalo, bulls, and other animals snort and stomp the ground with their feet when we approach?

Watch one of your pets and see if you can understand what it is trying to say. Write down the sounds and draw the postures that you see, then record what they mean. Why does your dog sometimes greet you with tail wagging, while at other times its tail is tucked between its legs? Why does your cat rub its mouth against walls and furniture, or circle and look up at you when you walk in the door? What do you do and say to communicate with your pet? You are learning to speak and understand another creature's language.

Animals "speak" to us in different ways. When we see that a certain kind of insect, bird, or mammal is disappearing from its natural home, that animal is "telling" us that something is wrong. This is another way to read the language of the animals.

Talk to your parents, grandparents, and other elders and ask them which animals were common when they were your age. Are those animals still common? If not, why not?

Keep an eye on the animals and animal homes around you to see if anything is changing. Maybe the soil or water has been polluted, the forest has been cut down, or someone is hunting or collecting too many of a certain kind of animal. Tell your friends, classmates, and family what is happening. What do you think those changes will mean for the well-being of the animals? Is there anything that you, and others, can do about it? If so, then take action!

Trees of Life, Roots of Faith

(Genesis 2:9–10, Isaiah 41:17–20, & Ezekiel 17:1–10, 22–24)

The Lord God made trees spring forth from the soil in the Garden of Eden. Beautiful trees grew there, trees whose branches bore fruit, nuts, and all good things to eat. In the middle of the Garden, God planted the most magnificent tree of all. It was the Tree of Life, whose fruit was the knowing of good and evil. From the roots of the Tree of Life arose a river of cool and clear water. Down into the valley the river flowed and branched into four streams that coursed through the rich lands that lay before the Lord at the beginning of time.

"When the oppressed and the poor are thirsty and can find no water, and their tongues are parched, I will come to help them," said the Lord, "for I am the God of Israel. Out of the dunes of desert sands, and from the wells in the valleys, I will cause rivers to flow. Pools will appear in the wilderness and fresh springs will bubble up from dry land.

"Out in the wastelands I will plant cedar trees and acacia, myrtle and wild olive. In the barren scrub I will plant pines that will grow tall amid boxwood and fir.

"All people who witness these forests and greening of the land will know and understand what the Lord alone has created, that the Holy One of Israel has done these great acts.

"I will reach down with my hand and prune a sprig from the top of the great cedar and I will plant it in the earth. I will take a fresh green bud from the highest branch and set it in the soil on the top of the loftiest mountain in Israel. There it will grow and branch into the thick crown of a noble cedar rich with fruit. Birds of all kinds will come to roost in its arching branches and in the cool shade of its leaves. The great boughs will protect them.

"Every tree that grows in this land will know the power of God. I alone can bring down the tops of mighty trees and make short trees tall. I can cause green leaves to dry up and die, and can create new growth from withered branches. What I, the Lord, have said this day, so I will do."

One day, the Lord God spoke to the Israelites and told them this parable: A magnificent eagle, with great wings and long talons and feathers of many colors and delicate designs, flew to Lebanon. There he gripped the top of a cedar tree in his great claws, bore it away to a prosperous city, and planted the tree in this new land.

Time passed and the eagle planted again. This time it planted a seed in the fresh, rich earth by a river where its roots would have plenty of water. While the eagle stood on the soil above, the seed grew into a strong vine that spread along the ground. Its shoots and tendrils reached toward the eagle and its roots grew beneath his feet. In time it branched out, bore fruit, and grew into a noble vine.

Then another powerful eagle, with wings wide and feathers strong, landed along the shore of the river. The roots of the vine began to grow toward this new eagle and its branches spread to where the eagle perched. As it grew farther from the soil where its seed had first sprouted, the roots of the vine became shallow, the branches thin and tangled, and the leaves began to wither.

A vine cannot be strong and survive if it is divided and grows in two directions. It will be easily uprooted and stolen. Its roots will break and its fruit taken. When the east wind blows, its leaves will wither, then the vine shall wilt and die where it once flourished.

Reflections

In the first story, trees are a gift from God—their branches bear a bounty of foods to eat and their beauty enriches our souls. Birds are like jewels in the branches of trees. Trees are symbols of God's creative powers and generosity and a reminder of God's hold over the forces of nature. Water begins to flow in the desert; it nurtures the roots of cedar, olive, and other trees God plants in the wild places. A river flows from the roots of the Tree of Life in the Garden of Eden and branches into four streams that course over the land.

It is not surprising that a river flows from the roots of the Tree of Life. In nature, trees protect the soil and the waters that flow through the forest. Roots hold the soil in place and prevent erosion along the riverbanks. In this way forests help to keep our streams and rivers clean and clear.

Trees shade the waters and create a cool home for fish and other aquatic life. Leaves also cast shade on the forest floor and cover the ground with a spongy layer that absorbs rainwater. When forests are cleared, the soil heats up and dries out. Rain runs off quickly, which carries soil away and pollutes the water. The heat and dryness that come when forests are cut can cause streams and rivers to disappear.

Trees play an important role in many stories of the Bible. It is clear in the stories from Isaiah and Ezekiel that God is proud of trees and uses them as symbols of both the power of Creation and of what God has given to the people. Roots can teach us about the strength of our faith. In Ezekiel, the roots of the vine are fed by the soil beneath the eagle that planted it. When a second eagle comes, the roots split and grow toward that eagle. If we are not careful, our faith, too, can become divided and weak, like the roots of the vine. We need to sink our roots deep and keep our faith strong.

When we try to do too many things, our energy and attention become divided and we can lose sight of our original goals. Our busy lives are like a vine that grows in many directions at once. At times we need to do some careful pruning so that we may focus, grow strong, and bear fruit.

Activities

If the Bible were a color, it would have to be green. From the olive leaf that the dove brings back to Noah aboard the ark to the famous cedar of Lebanon, from pomegranate to fig and palm, the roots of trees and other kinds of plants weave through the Bible like green fingers of life. Here are some of the plants that grow in the stories of the scriptures:

Trees and Shrubs

acacia tree

almond tree

almug or algum tree

bay tree (laurel leaf)

box tree

carob

cassia

cedar of Lebanon

cinnamon tree

date palm

fig tree

hyssop plant

juniper (Rethem) or white broom

mastic tree

mustard tree (toothbrush tree or arak tree)

myrrh

myrtle tree

olive tree

pistachio nut

pomegranate tree

rose of Sharon

spikenard

sycamore tree

walnut tree

weeping willow

willow

Grains, Herbs, and Flowers

anise

barley

coriander

cummin (black cumin or fitches)

flax

lentiles

lily (scarlet martagon or red Turk's-cap lily)

mandrake (dudaim)

millet

mustard (black)

rye

saffron

tares

wheat

Plants of the Bible

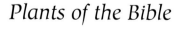

MATERIALS: Bible, paper, pencil, encyclopedia, crayons, pictures or photographs of trees in the Bible, one copy of the *I Am a _____ Tree* story, music player and recording of classical music, seeds from your favorite tree, small shovel, watering can.

Read several Bible stories in which trees appear and write down the names of those trees. Look up the trees in an encyclopedia, or on the World Wide Web. Some good website search engines to consult are MSN.com, Netscape.com, and Google.com. Consult the list of endangered species and their descriptions at this location on line: ECES (EarthCrash EarthSpirit). Also, call up WebBible.net and look under "Plants of the Bible."

Find as many pictures or photographs of the trees as you can. Draw some pictures of those trees and pick out one that you like the best. Write the name of that tree into the blank spaces in the following story, then imagine you *are* that tree as you read the story.

I AM A _____ TREE

Back when I was young, my seed fell from a branch and dropped to the ground. For many weeks I lay there, afraid that someone would come along and step on me or eat me.

One day, a squirrel gathered me into its mouth, carried me away, and buried me in the ground. In the dark, cool soil my shell split open and I started to sprout. A tiny root reached down and began to gather food and water from the soil. A pale sprout came out of my shell. The sprout grew and grew until it broke through the top of the soil and into the bright sunlight. Then I spread my young leaves and felt the warm sun for the first time.

Each day the sun's rays warmed my leaves and gave me the energy to grow. I became taller and taller as my stems grew more and more leaves.

Late one night, a large animal came and chewed off some of my buds. And I kept growing. Another time, some people walking by broke off some of my branches and used them to make a cooking fire. And still I grew. Birds, squirrels, and many other animals ate the nuts that formed on my twigs. A strong wind blew down one of my branches and when the dry seasons came, my leaves fell off, so I went to sleep until the rains returned. But year after year my crown of leaves just kept getting higher and wider.

Now I am a tall _____ tree whose branches spread far from my trunk and reach up toward the sky. If you ever walk by me along the trail, don't forget to say hello and to thank me for my cool shade. God has given me many wonderful gifts, and I have shared them with others. One of these days, I will share them with you.

All of God's Creation is alive. Plants hear what we say to them and they grow stronger when we speak kindly and play gentle, soothing tunes, especially classical music. Bring a portable music player and a classical recording and visit one of your favorite trees. Sit down with your back against the tree's trunk. Read the second paragraph in the *Reflections* section of this chapter and think about the good things that trees do for the forests, for the soil, and for our rivers and streams. Say thank you for the many things the tree has given to you, then play the music and say, "And here is a gift that I return to you."

When the seeds of your favorite trees are ripe, take several of the seeds home, plant them around your home, and water them. Take care of the young trees when they sprout and, if you're careful, you will have offshoots of your favorite tree growing in your own yard. A useful book to read is *Flowers, Trees, and Fruits* by Sally Morgan (New York: Larousse, Kingfisher Chambers, Inc., 2002).

Touching Trees

MATERIALS: A long piece of rope, blindfolds.

Go with your family, class, or some friends to a pine grove, hardwood forest, or park where there are many large, old trees. Send one person out ahead of the others and have them tie one end of a long rope to a tree. That person will then create a trail by leading the rope from tree to tree, wrapping it around each tree along the way, and then tying it off to the last tree.

The leader will blindfold the first person in the group and lead that person to the first tree. The blindfolded person will spend time feeling the bark, roots, branches, and leaves of that first tree before moving along the guide rope to the next tree. At one of the trees, the leader will say, "This is your tree, so touch it carefully and remember each bump, crack, branch, and root." At the end of the rope walk, the blindfolded person must take off the blindfold and go back to find her or his own tree.

Now have the person who was just blindfolded become the leader and lead someone else along the walk. Keep leading each other and switching roles until everyone has had a chance to both lead and find during the Touching Trees walk.

Trees of Faith

Trees grow rooted in one place for their entire lives and often live for a hundred years or more. Giant Sequoias can survive for more than 3200 years and some bristlecone pines—the oldest trees on Earth—are over 4600 years old! Trees become deeply connected to the place where they live. As time passes, trees grow closely with the soil and things that live in the ground. If we are to understand trees, it is important to treat them like the living things they are and to try and experience the world from *their* point of view. By imagining the life of a tree, we can come closer to God.

MATERIALS: Mats to sit on, hand lenses, ball of thick white string, blunt-tipped scissors, pieces of construction paper, and either a pen, pencil, or marker with which to write poems, songs, or Bible stories about trees.

Ask a group of friends, family, or classmates to find a poem, song, or Bible story about trees that they would want to read, sing, or play to the tree you will visit. Have each person bring something that fits for them so they won't feel foolish.

Go as a group to a forest or wooded park setting and bring the things you gathered to share with a tree. Wander around for a while until the group discovers a tree that they want to sit under and share with.

Have everyone sit in a circle and share their readings. Then take turns reading the Bible stories that are at the beginning of this section. Ask the group, "What do these readings and stories mean to you?" Allow time for everyone to respond.

Now take some time to look through a hand lens at the bark, leaves, and seeds of the tree. Then focus on the lichens, mosses, and other living things that are part of the community that grows on, in, and around your tree.

One lesson that comes from these stories is that trees are powerful symbols of God's creative powers. They are living examples of God's love and generosity. Trees are sacred in the eyes of God; they are an important part of Creation, just like people. Ask the group, "What does this mean about the way we treat trees?"

Take a ball of white string and cut off several pieces. Lay these down on the ground to symbolize roots. Use a long piece and run it up and down, or back and forth many times to create the trunk. Take another long piece and make the outline of a treetop.

Cut some pieces of construction paper into quarters. Start at the bottom and ask, "What are the roots of our faith?" Write down each of these responses on a piece of construction paper and place each one at the end of a root. "What holds our faith up?" Place these answers along the trunk. "What are the flowers, fruits, and seeds that we grow by living our faith?" Scatter these in the tree's crown. When you are done, take a few minutes to discuss the thoughts and ideas that everyone has just shared.

Glossary

covenant   An unbreakable promise or agreement.

cubit   An ancient measurement taken from the tip of the middle finger to the elbow. One cubit equals about 20 inches.

diversity   The number of different kinds of plants and animals, and the number of each kind, that live in a particular place.

endangered species   A species that has so few members left that it is in danger of becoming extinct.

habitat   The forest, desert, ocean, river, field, pond, or other place where a particular plant or animal lives.

haiku   A form of Japanese poetry that does not rhyme. The first and last of the three lines have five syllables and the second line has seven syllables.

Nephilim   Giants—biblical beings who did deeds of greatness and heroism in the early days of Creation.

stewardship   To protect and take care of plants, animals, people, and all of God's Creation—Earth and Sky. To do God's will in service to nature and humankind.

talons   The sharp, curved claws on a bird of prey or *raptor*.

Yahweh (Jehovah)   God.